GW00597214

Love's First Look

The Poetics of Contemplation 1

Love's First Look

Collected Poems, S. C. Fordham
2007 to 2010

'a shelter, a resting place
in which to ignite the fire
and burn
in which to let the light in after dark
and learn'

The Poetics of Contemplation 1, Love's First Look, Collected Poems by S. C. Fordham
2007 to 2010, published by S. C. Fordham in 2010
© S. C. Fordham 2010
Author's Preface © Sarah Fordham 2010
Foreword © Faith Forster 2010

All material quoted from the Bible is taken from the New American Standard Bible

The right of Sarah Fordham to be identified as the author of this work has been asserted by her in accordance with the Copyright, Designs and Patents Act 1988.

All rights reserved. No part of this publication may be reproduced, stored in a retrieval system, or transmitted, in any form or by any means, electronic, mechanical, photocopying, recording or otherwise, without the prior permission of the copyright owner.

A CIP catalogue record of this book is available from the British Library.

ISBN 978-0-9563219-1-6

Designed and produced in the UK by KSD Associates Ltd
ksdassociates.co.uk

Edited by Jenny Page

Printed in Great Britain by the MPG Books Group, Bodmin and King's Lynn

For further information please email Sarah Fordham at sarah.fordham@btinternet.com

http://blogspot.scfordham.com

Human beings, in a certain sense, are unknown to themselves. Jesus Christ not only reveals God, but 'fully reveals man to man'. In Christ, God has reconciled the world to himself. All believers are called to bear witness to this; but it is up to you, men and women who have given your lives to art, to declare with all the wealth of your ingenuity that in Christ the world is redeemed: the human person is redeemed, the human body is redeemed, and the whole creation which, according to Saint Paul, 'awaits impatiently the revelation of the children of God' (Romans 8 v. 19), is redeemed. The creation awaits the revelation of the children of God also through art and in art. This is your task. Humanity in every age, and even today, looks to works of art to shed light upon its path and its destiny.

from Letter to Artists, *Pope John Paul I I*

For now we see in a mirror dimly, but then face to face; now I know in part, but then I shall know fully, just as I have been fully known.

I Corinthians 13 v. 12

Contents

Foreword

This book of poetry is full of good, truth-filled words: words woven lightly, forming poems of short, beautiful simplicity, as in 'The Sound of the Sea', and words woven darkly and deeply as in 'The Scourging'. Sometimes the words weave a story, a dramatic picture, as in 'Blood Brother's Blood'. Each poem needs to be savoured for its own encapsulation of truth or beauty.

Sarah's poetic expressions range from musing on her own deep thoughts, to a lifting up of her eyes (and ours) to the lofty heights of enduring truth and the revelation of the eternal. This weaving together of external and internal revelation is very characteristic of Sarah's writings, together with her empathic ability to discern and express the feelings of others, as well as her own.

Sarah has been a part of Ichthus Christian Fellowship for many years, and represents us on various ecumenical groups. She manages to combine a love of spirituality with a commitment to practical action for the world's poor through her work with Integral, a global alliance of Christian relief and development agencies.

There are too few passionate people in the world. Most of us could echo the feeling expressed in Shakespeare's lines: 'Tomorrow, and tomorrow and tomorrow, Creeps in this petty pace from day to day . . . ' In the mundane of life, we simply miss the jewels. Sarah has an instinct, a perceptiveness and a passion not only to notice the jewels but to gather them so that we may see them too. In essence, that is what she has done in Love's First Look. Read and enjoy!

Faith Forster
London, October 2010

Author's Preface

My strongest desire in writing poetry has always been to make the truest possible transcript in poetic form of my emotions, lived out as they are in my experience.

Within the Christian narrative there is a tremendous promise of unveiling and beholding. I believe it is not only in death or at Christ's return that we will see the Lord of glory, but that we can see Him today, if we can only hold His gaze. When Jesus was on the earth He looked at many people – the poor, the sick, the lost, prostitutes and criminals, the proud and the rich, His family and His disciples. Some of them returned His gaze and did not look away from Him for the rest of their lives. Some turned away from Him for a time, pained by their own sense of failure. Still others dismissed Him, not giving Him a second glance. These choices are also our own.

Why do we so often avert our eyes? In John's Gospel, chapter six it says that many of Jesus' disciples withdrew and were not walking with Him any more. This caused Jesus to ask His disciples, 'You do not want to go away also, do you?' Simon Peter, one of twelve closest to Jesus, who went on to deny Him as the cock crowed, answered, 'Lord, to whom shall we go? You have words of eternal life. We have believed and have come to know that You are the Holy One of God.'

Jesus' reply to Simon Peter reveals that He is thinking of Judas, the one who will so terribly betray Him with that brazen kiss. If I had to cite the poem that is the symbolic centre of this collection, and perhaps my entire work, it would be *The Price of Blood*. John's gospel tells us that when Judas went out, 'it was night'. The tragic drama of the one never to return always stops me in my tracks and causes me to reflect on where I am with Jesus. Have I betrayed the Lord? Am I betraying Him? Or am I committed to staying with Him, holding His gaze no matter what?

The statement 'God is love' means that the only relationship possible with God is one of Lover and Beloved; and this is why we betray Him every time we turn away from Him, not knowing then what it is only possible to know afterwards – that there is only emptiness and restlessness in going out to a 'far country'. Just as the father in the parable of the Prodigal Son waits patiently for his child to come to his senses, so God, full of a longing that is difficult for us to imagine, scans the horizon to catch that first glimpse of us, His weary wanderers. And what a celebration awaits us, who, like the Prodigal Son, 'was dead but has begun to live, and who was lost and has been found'.

Beholding is a theme also woven through my first collection of poems, *The Cool of the Day*. In my poem 'Who? When? Where? Why? What?' I ask, 'Can I hold your gaze for a lifetime?' This thought returns in different ways throughout that collection ('Forgive me / if I cannot stand / on the banks / of fathomless love'). However, many of the poems in *The Cool of the Day* have a different tone, being written in the first half of my life when the sun was still high in my sky. As it now passes its zenith, shadows lengthen … *Love's First Look* is a more contemplative collection, experiential as well as experimental, an attempt to get 'under the surface' of the Christian life in order to explore its depths. They may be my depths, but I offer my poems to you in the hope that there are points of connection along the way, particularly for those who are yet to enter, or still to return to the house that has been so lovingly and lavishly prepared for them.

Sarah Fordham
October 2010, London

Time's Passing

I am
A running brook
Stones in your heart made smooth
A wound in the landscape winding
On through

I am
A still small voice
Whispers of night return
The longing of day swept away
My love

I call
Revealed at last
Sun, moon and starry sky
The clouds, they are parted for us
So come

In peace
Resting at dusk
So many underground
Where do we begin to recall
What's lost

What's found
What's fashioned us
What will awaken us
What has surrounded the echo
Of dawn

i trace myself back . . .

i trace myself back
through time's shell
i gather silence to dwell within

my darling heart
beats still . . .
i am over here

let me be a window
to let the light in
before dark

love, it's getting late
time is quickening
and tracing back so faint

slower now
more deliberate
i look at you

my words
fall, falling
like soft rain . . .

upon skin
upon stone
upon hearts

and i trace . . .
time's shell
. . . to therein dwell

The Human Family

Marked for a tribal future.
The face of a stranger appears in a dream;
And then fades into a forgetting day.

What breath, what breeze
Could change our fate?

Clothed in kindred spirits.
The face of Mother like the sun never to set;
Nothing to be seen in the glare.

What war, what want
Could change our minds?

Driven by a need so deep.
It's never to be named, not to be met;
Pushing down, down into dust.

What rhetoric, what ritual
Could change our hearts?

Marked. A bloody future.
Subsumed by the wounds of a stranger;
Scars. Remembrance. The Human Family.

dogs of war

dogs of war are fighting on
our hearts full of pity
for kids with no hands to hold
no feet to run and tell
of nasty dreams and screams
who will turn you in?
you curs of the world
you curse us
barking at the broken dawn
we stare into the night
you lick your silver and gold
have your bloody feasts
and god knows what is
unleashed

treatise

unmet vows are sworn
into the night sky
they gather towards
one bleeding dawn
so many promises broken
as morning scatters holy wars
wholly yours, wholly mine
hurry away, my love
the time dies
rest will not kiss you
see the horizon
and not the demise
beauty still marches
truth stands silently
goodness has vanished
but we remain
mouthing
'no more, no more war'
some still say it's a just
expression of man's aggression
as his hands drip sores
in the wet garden
the story unfolds
the plot is a forest
in which many are lost
woe-filled worlds collide
the end is an arrow
right through my heart
my love, please hide
how will we break
the back of despair?
pray and weep with me
for warfare is made
choice is before us
his feet are passing
my man, where are you?
rest in my shade

Dictator

Dictator,
Were you a boy who played in trees,
Ran down dusty lanes so as not to be late for tea?

Dictator,
I hide and am hungry.
I dare not run far for a mine may greet me before Mother.

Dictator,
You live behind such high gates,
While a slow death march into terror's marsh is my fate.

Dictator,
Did you dream as a boy,
And wake needing a father's hand on your shoulder?

Dictator,
I can no longer remember the features of my father's face.
Your image fills my every waking moment.

Dictator,
I am so small.
Your power is a fast-flowing river full of bodies.

Dictator,
What do you recall tonight,
As the wind blows through the dry grasses?

Dictator,
I wanted to be a doctor,
A ship's captain, an explorer, a pilot . . .

Dictator,
I wanted to be a teacher, a builder of houses, a writer . . .
Anything, anything at all, but not, never, ever, a freedom-fighter.

shooting star

fallen to earth
shards of light at my heels
all mine

Too Much

The birds call to each other
The branches are bare
The frosty night governs the land
The birds twitter and then there is silence

The ancient poet said, 'Let silence take you to the core of life'*

What can be melted down and remade?
Lies liquidised and traded in
Love solidified and given out with the instruction:

You must end the search for happiness

Too much to stop
Too much to want to see the signpost pointing away from home
Too much water under the bridge not to be carried along by the past's
        dark tide
Too much agony, too much destiny
Too much talk to hear . . .

Within the still small centre hides the reactor that locates the power

. . .

Centre of the earth
Centre of my soul

. . .

There is too much to know

* Rumi

summer of my life

i recall the sand – the cliffs – the strong tides
the rocks – the walks – the fire in the year of drought
walking quickly through thick smoke
so as not to get licked – hot tongues
panting for water and for love

the descent into autumn is not as i thought
a movement of leaves – winds – the sober colours of dying
who calls – who sees – who knows what winter will be
spring will not come again
and the summer, the summer is gone

The Ravine of Kidron

–The inner vision of a cup
Pleased to crush –

Strength from above
Pressed on every side
Life blood squeezed out
One drop of a bloody
Tide to flow

One betraying
As footsteps fill the air
Torches, lanterns, weapons
To extinguish
The world's light

Taken down with a kiss
A sword's flash
A severed ear
And one final miracle
In the garden of your circle
– Breaking –

Pleased to crush –
–The inner vision of a cup

John 18 vs 1–11
Isaiah 53 v. 5

After long night, up-risen is the morn

After shock, silence
After silence, speech

After speech, sleep
After sleep, seek

After long night
Up-risen is the morn

Mourn dark days
Up-rise the tide of dawn

Spectacle

This is not the time to come clean
This is not the time to be seen

Come out of the shadows
Lift up your eyes to the hills
A helper comes

This is the time of clouds
The opening of heaven's gate

People are dying
Slower than a fading star

People are living
Faster than a speeding bullet

The body cannot bear for too long

Bereavement
Betrayal
A brave face
Torture
Solitary confinement
The flow of water and of memory
Questions unanswered and unseeking
The eye of the storm
Sadness entering the soul
Unending snowfall
Relentless sunshine
Waterless places
Lovelessness
Foodlessness
Homelessness
A diet of carelessness and control
Tiredness and loneliness and bloodshed
A slow heartbeat or a fast one
Or impact
Or dictatorships
Obscenity or obesity
Trivia or tireless complexity
Concrete
The colour grey
Confusion
Negation
No touch
No air
No light
Nonsense
There are many, many things under heaven that a body cannot bear for too
long
Start your own list
Publish the findings
Call a summit
Deprivation and excess are crimes against humanity <> perpetual death

The soul cannot bear for too long

Reality TV
Breakfast TV
Celebrity

Free papers
News obsession
Tabloid lying

No good thought
No good word
No good act

No art
No passion
No pain

Memorise the few things that the soul cannot bear for too long
So as to avoid a slow, slow death
Rehearse them every morning while looking in the mirror
Because they are easily forgotten and very, very hard to resist

The spirit cannot bear for too long

Prostitution
Adultery
Promiscuity
Idolatry

Deception

Forbidden fruit poisons
And the death that follows is very, very quick

Belshazzar's Feast

I set a place of forgetting at the table.
It was only after the meal that I remembered,
And then it was too late . . .

the sound of the sea

the roar drowns out all other sound
coming from fathoms away towards shore
i am fishing today for what was lost
generations before

time is a measure equal to none

running out, passing by, catching up
fixed, moving, marked
captured is what i am
an hourglass containing
many grains slipping
through various fingers

closing eyes
counting to ten
time hides and seeks
and always finds
the crack in the armour
the chink in the chain

People of the Time

Open your mouth to say what?
These days people speak, I speak, too often only to self

Open your ears to hear what?
Indistinct words, lies or a reputation being trashed

Open your eyes to see what?
Flesh lifted on high, daily to be devoured

Open your mind to understand what?
Crashing stocks, life through the lens, the crying of the war-torn, died too
    soon

Open your heart to feel what?
Emptiness that whirls you in an endless dance

Open your closed door to what?
The entrance of sorrow

Like candles flickering in remote outposts
We give light only to our fantasies

But sometimes when it is very quiet
A whisper from the mountain's edge can be heard

Open only once – to speak, to hear, to see, to understand, to feel
The other side of fear; which is faith

After-word

When it was all over I asked the wisest man I could find which way to go.
He looked me straight in the heart and said, 'Stay right here and let the
silence fill you.'

internal elements

earth
mixed in my hands

fire
smouldered in my heart

air
swirled in my lungs

water
seeped from my eyes

life
radiated outwards

elemental
words fail me

inside
i've taken it all

God ...

... The rock from which I was hewn
The quarry from which I was dug

Abraham my father
Sarah my mother

My desert a garden
Joy and gladness found

Waste places comforted
Melodious sound

Isaiah 51 vs 1–3

turning of a season

swiftly summer light descends into autumn breeze
beloved, tell me what i cannot see
as the leaves are falling from the trees

Spring in Winter

My heart is not afraid any more
My eyes are not dazzled by the glitz and glamour of this world
Blinded by the clamour
Or clouded by the judgements of others

I do not presume, assume, consume
Or take for granted any more
God's lovingkindness and compassion

I give space to my soul's expression
My soul is like newly washed curtains that I must draw at nightfall
So I can abide, confide, not strive
And open them again at the dawning of a new day

This causes me to come and go with rejoicing
A spring in my step though it be winter all around

In my travelling, arriving, waiting, returning or departing
There is a distance to cross
A journey, a race, a destination to reach
A space to exist within

At last
It's in the palm of his hand

And of my weeping something has been left, which must now die*

And of my weeping something has been left, which must now die
Tell me when, how much
Sorry eyes have taken in, and then repelled
There is no evening sorrow too soon or slow, for love's door
Dream again now, night comes sure
Empty-armed, enfolded, sleep tight my love
The morning will beckon us once more
First light is in our breaking

what broke u down vain citadels?*

what broke u down vain citadels?
winter underfoot and cold, cold hands
empty eyes and a fierce wind from the east
defying any notion of a loving god

what broke u down lost girl?
vanity, vanity chirps the bird
cheap, cheap mourns the flesh
melding with god knows what

what broke u down dreamer?
one figment too many rose up
to offer your destiny on past's plate
eat, eat now and sleep as you wake

what broke me down?
winter, cold hands, empty eyes
the east wind, vanity, mourning
and today's dreams of yesterday

*Titles from poems by Wilfred Owen

from what well was i drawn?

water mixed with earth
my earth, your earth

the dug place
where longing mingled

with instinct
and i was born

bloody, brown, beheld
within a broken morn

from what well was i drawn?
from what touch did i ignite?

flaming passion dawns
my love, your love

my fire, your air
all the elements there

all our dreams held
trembling, barely remembered

glimpsed in the uneven surface
of the deep, deep well

forgive me but i cannot give
what i cannot hold

the reasoning of my birth
water mixed with earth

the well is primeval
primordial, instinctive

i dive to die
i die to live

water mixed with blood
the earth spins, screams

as sin is blinded
by the light of another world

blazing new birth is the beginning
of a new heaven, a new earth

from what well was i drawn?
the depths of your eyes

your fathomless
incalculable loss

banner

peace settled after battle's edge had been blunted
and there was no wind from north, south, east or west
baby hushed, mama gone and hand raised like a flag to herald victory's song

symbolic competency has left the building

no metaphor
no meter
no structure
no rhythm
no rhyme

no symbol
no analogy
no methodology
no competency
no language

no substance
no reality
no reason
no rhythm
no rhyme

no learning
no leaning
no receiving
no giving
no believing

no identity
no fluidity
no reason
no rhythm
no rhyme

words
but no reading
sound
but no hearing
sight
but no beholding

no thanks
no gift
no giver
no presence
no one

empty
outside
but full
of meaning
within

tonight
only
contemplation
is home

We may be delivering a monologue out of despair, with no listener in sight, but silence will absorb it and change it into a dialogue at some point in the continuum of the future. In this lies hope. For the obscure gaps, whether in life or in art, need not be as frightening as a precipice. The drama of existence is not all voice. Nor is it voice heard only at a given time. It has its silences, pauses, and gestures in lieu of words.

From The Other Side of Silence – The Poet at the Limit of Language by
Jerzy Peterkiewicz

The Winter Garden

On through the shaky gate
To tread upon the makeshift bridge
I won't look down in case I trip
Perhaps I'll glimpse the former garden glory in the parting of the branches
    of the still strong trees
Perhaps I'll hear the fountain's call in the falling of the rain upon the stones
    that have remained

And in between the weeds and waste
And even in the watches of the night
The ancient gardener waits and sees, and knows when the planting time is right
With such skilled hands, soil-encased, made rough by wood and work
He bends, whispering words of love to seeds unseen
For he knows, he knows the garden's song unsung
And smiles, for the winter flowering, it has begun

the poetics of contemplation

cycles, profiles
reiteration, repetition, reinterpretation, recurring themes, repeating images
thought poised on thought
sudden leaps into paradox, the paradox of negation
inscape
monologue, implied dialogue, speaking through an adopted character,
articulating the struggle for self-knowledge, segments of conversation
embedded in the text without formal indication that they are dialogue,
sequences of thought presented as conversations with oneself, *inner
dialogue implied* [ ] –
overlapping questions and answers, double-edged questions
the subject and object uniting, the medium and the message converging
compact phrases, as well as long, long lines …
the poetics of contemplation, the frontier of language redefined
an invitation, a welcome, a greeting – *please, my love* – *come inside*

Blood Brother's Blood

My blood boiled
It was so hot out there in the field tilling and tilling
Spilling my sweat to soften Mama and Papa's curse
Attached to me before my birthing, hardly fair
Kicking and screaming, they said, I emerged
A blinking man-child into a new day dawning
So bad it was, they said, God Almighty himself had to help
Get me out

Believe me
It wasn't easy extracting life from out of that damned earth
That bloody fruit will hang over me to my dying day
A sign of my inadequacy
Dripping with jealous juice for him, younger smug son
Striving always I was, am still, a man for all seasons
Hands bleeding at nightfall
Feet caked in mud

My offering was born of my bent back
I was never good enough
Not for them, or for him or for God Almighty
I tried, I really did, to sing his praises
But would feel Father's steel gaze boring into my skull
In the sweltering heat
It made me so, so mad
They all knew, all of them, what my offering was really made of

Even the livestock skipping in golden boy's field knew it
So snug in their animal skins
No wonder my countenance fell when God Almighty leaned towards him
Lazing, gazing upon his grazing stock
While I kissed the dismal dust
No wonder sin pounced and devoured
What was left of my God-given goodness
You must master it?

You mayest master it?
My choice to open the door and unleash that sharp-toothed dog?
My choice to murder my God-given brother?
However, my résumé *is* noteworthy
I was the one who lived despite my dogged early years
A vagrant, a wanderer, climbed the ladder to be the first city's builder
Father of culture, a murderer marked by God's mercy
A workaholic

And humanity unfurled from my line, *mine*
But in rising early and sleeping so little, so late
I'd hear my pumping red heart by day
In the beating of the steel
In the sharpening of spears
But at night in restless slumber I'd know what was the sound
It was my blood brother's blood crying out for vengeance
From that damned bloody curse of my ground

Genesis 4 vs 1–16

What will I do no matter what?

When nothing has worked out and I'm counting the cost,
I'll write my own psalm, picture your dark garden night and the silver
    gleaming in Judas's palm.

When the day has closed in around my heart and I'm squeezed into a tight spot,
I'll close my eyes, and ask for the passing of the cup.

When I cannot face what it is I need to do,
I'll get up, lock my door and make my way to your house.

When I can't hear you, I'll keep speaking.
When I can't feel you, I'll take the bread.

When I can't see you, I'll clasp the cup.
No matter what. No matter what.

When nothing has worked out and I'm counting the cost,
I'll write my own psalm, picture your dark garden night and the silver
    gleaming in Judas's palm.

The Scourging

Prince of Peace made a scourge of cords to drive them all out
The thieves with murder in their eyes
The murderers with money in their fists
Overturner of corruption, by zeal consumed
For what your Father's house had become
Prayer exchanged for trade

Eternal truth for material gain
Man, the measure of all; God, the judge of all
Meeting in you; your hands and feet moving
So fast, to make it all stop
Perhaps you were thinking of your thieving betrayer
Empty-fisted, to swing in the field of silver

Or your scourging to be meted out by your amoral judge
Or the robber they would let go, or the two thieves
You would spend your last moments between
But here, here was power to make a clean sweep
Of indifference, compromise, injustice
To use your hands and feet, so soon to be pinned down

Defiantly, definitely, deftly to make swift what was required
Mercy, not sacrifice; justice as a fast-flowing stream
My Lord, it was to the sellers of doves that you spoke
I imagine tears behind your eyes, scourge of cords in your hand
Dust on your feet, and passion burning in your heart
For this, your Father's only earthly house

And the judgement, the judgement was made
As the coins fell through the air; the glory departed
The temple, soon to be razed to the ground
The temple, a structure thus doomed
The temple, now embodied in a human frame
And death, yours and mine, to be consumed

John 2 vs 13–21

The Price of Blood

How do we betray?

How do we turn from the Good?

Exchange the True for vapour,

And so hurriedly hide Beauty's face?

Why can we not stay?

What moves us away?

How do we forsake so quickly the Forsaken One?

Track through the darkness to nowhere so fast

And so soon evening falls with those thirty pieces of silver

Onto the temple sanctuary stone

How do we betray?

Remorse swelling in the secret chamber, swirling

Nowhere to go, nowhere to hide

Judas didn't flee to God

Judas didn't fall to his knees

The chief priests and elders might as well have been made

Of that sanctuary stone

Judas's confession fell in the fading light upon the ears

Of unrelenting, unforgiving selfhood

What is that to us? See to that yourself ...

Where else was there to go?

Jesus hand and foot was bound

Friend, do what you have come for ...

Tell me, how do we betray?

And when it's done there's a mighty flood no man can stop

The price of blood set by Israel's sons

O tell me, why do we betray?

Thirty pieces of silver shining in the moonlight

The Lord's blood bought

What is our price?

What have we paid?

Blood to cover the earth and all that man has made

In every place; brought back that day

As all of God's wealth slipped through his fingers

Did we not see the grave danger?

The burial place for strangers emitting a reddish glow

In the receding sun

With Israel's son, apostate

Swinging in the breeze

Of unrelenting, unforgiving selfhood

Matthew 27 vs 1–10
Acts 1 v. 20

The days are falling from the trees

In such silence I hide,
a leaf released from the wind,
no longer anxious for the days that fall.
They must all fall. I know.

   Karol Wojtyla, from Song of the Hidden God

The days are falling from the trees
Curled at the edges, different colours covering the ground
And with the days tumble words of many kinds
Strong, sad, simple; forming piles to kick up
And discover the deepest meaning
Of the trunk of self as it irrevocably sheds its load

The days are falling from the trees
The letting-go of love in the gentle breeze
A display of many-shaded brightness before
The stripping bare comes, comes slow
And then the downpour, and then the stillness
Of winter pressing up against the soul

The days are falling from the trees
Revealing the structure bare against the skyline
The disintegrating heaps of weeks, months, years all mine
To have wasted, worked, whispered the wisdom
Stored in the roots, beneath bark, the rings within
Lord, may I be fully alive at the extremities until the final leaf falls

My God, I'm Free

I'm free not to look within or without or around
I'm free to feed whatsoever I choose, drive myself underground
I'm free to uphold my word and my power however I like
I'm free to hide or unveil my notion of self, shivering or sweating it doesn't matter
I'm free to descend into blind imagination, interior darkness a curtain
    drawn across my soul's window
I'm free to be a widow tonight, grief at my fingertips infusing everything I touch
I'm free to twist, to beat, to turn figures of speech into towering
    archetypes to govern entire landscapes
I'm free to cast those shadows to the north, the south, the east, the west
I'm free to come back week after week – judge you, bring you down, vote
    you out
I'm free to change your destiny on the turning of my phrase
I'm free to reduce love to a set of hormonal responses
I'm free to relegate absolute essentials to the outer edges
I'm free to hedge my bets, say nothing to no one, listen to the silence and
    be comforted by the absence of presence

Remember Me

My words hanging in the air are like a knife
They cut me within like the nails piercing me without
Remember me when . . .
When I robbed, walked the streets as a robber
When I took all that I was and threw it to the dogs –
Covered by the night with a cloaked heart, it beats now
On high with you, amid the shouting, the jeering
The sneering crowd, but your eyes are beholding something else –
All that I never knew in this life; my last day is the same
As yours, King of the Jews; my sin, your shame
Your shame, my covering; I am uncloaked in your nakedness –
Remember me when you come in your kingdom . . .
The mist descending as the outline of another place takes shape
I never could have imagined such an end to my fate –
In the pain searing through my limbs, in my fading sight
In my dying breath to find life, and be with you today, Jesus, in paradise

Un-remembered

I was mad, suspended in time to die for my crimes
And I didn't give a damn, my guilt I considered of no account
I had taken what I needed, when I wanted it, it was my right
Nobody was going to give me anything and nobody ever proved me wrong
So I stole, and now I was left with only my bone-shaking vertical anger

I knew of this man hanging by my side
There was so much talk of him far and wide
Ha! Some sinless saviour, stripped and whipped
On the level with me now, I give him a sideways glance, a snipe
Somehow his serene stillness in the face of such searing pain

Drew the rage even more from every pore in my beaten body
I hated him as much as I hated myself, and this world
I had not asked to be born into, and this life I had no desire to live
I hurled abuse at him, the so-called king – are you not the Christ?
Save yourself and us, if you are this great deliverer, let us all off this bloody hook

And then my co-conspirator turned to address me: did I not fear God?
Was I not deserving of this condemnation? Did I not suffer rightly?
But this man had done nothing wrong . . . this man . . . who the hell was he?
What could he know of me?
I could not, would not let go of what had filled my every waking moment
      and fuelled my every single act

None of this was my fault – it was those rulers with their stone-cold eyes
Their silver-lined pockets and this so-called God who cared not to see
      what had been done to me
Today, who can tell me where I will be? No one. My lowered head
My closing eyes, the darkness welling up inside as the mist descends
If I was a praying man, my only plea would be that this was truly to be the end

Luke 23 vs 39–43

Jesus on the Cross

The tide signalled a special delivery.

Water flowed and soaked a small section of earth.

And then the blood. The birth.

Echoing still are the pangs, the labour and the cry to swallow up all cries.

The travail of one body held up high.

The final gasp, the opening of a wound. Such a public birth.

Can I call you Mother?

Scarred for all eternity.

I feel tonight the wood that your body pressed against for my birthing.

Your-spirit-given-up-into-greater-hands-and-another-kind-of-knowing.

A whole humanity formed within the womb of your mortal frame:

Brother-after-brother-after-sister-from-my-sacrificial-and-blessed-Mother.

Unconditional love. A life laid down . . .

Who could have imagined such a triumphal return, then, or through the piercing of time?

John, the Beheaded

What did we go out to see?
A reed bending and blowing in the wind of God's change
Billowing words from one stripped so bare
Marked by the desert and a message to pierce
Tyranny's rage, the oppression of a people
And a nation straining to see the dawning of humanity's final age

What did we go out to see?
A wilderness voice come home within the wildness of man's heart
Stirring the waters beneath in breathless anticipation of heaven's mighty
        waterfall
Dripping wet in a dry land, glistening golden in the noonday heat
Mercy making right, making straight the crooked way
For the Man, the Lamb, the taker of sin

What did we go out to see?
A man of fire who spoke of a greater burning to come
A man with a gaze to implant steel in the weakened backbone
Of a people waiting, whispering God's age-old promises
Of chosenness, closeness and covenant
Eyes fixed on the horizon to glimpse the appearing of the Father's only Son

What did we go out to see?
You knew who you were, recognised, prophesied, perceived the
            necessary increase and decrease
Felt your heart leap in greeting at last the sinless Saviour
Filled by the Holy Spirit in your mother's womb, now standing face to
            face with your mother's cousin's beloved Son
His beginning, the dove descending, did you know to herald your doom?

What did we go out to see?
A man cowed in prison, head in hands wondering how it came to this
Sunken in the pit of the king's darkened heart
Trampled under the sure-footed death dance of a hating queen
To be no more heard, thought severed, silence served up on that platter
An arm raised to fell the strong, tall prophet, who had so violently laid hold

What did we go out to see?
After everything, you asked your disciples to find out, was it he?
The blind now seeing, the deaf hearing, the dumb shouting praises, the
    poor lifted up; was it he?
What did you pray when you closed your eyes in that deep-down dark hell?
What did you hear? Did you speak as your executioner entered your cell?
John, the Baptiser, no less the voice of one crying in the wilderness as the
    blade rose, and then, so swiftly, fell

Flock

What was the sound between my first and last sight of day?
How could I speak what I had heard, and to whom?
Such whispers upon my breast, words like an immense flock of birds
Rising and falling, unbelievable patterns and intensity, so soon to vanish into dusk
Ascending or descending to who knows where, to who knows what . . .?

Love's First Look

My words were fading from me as the light diminished.

Reduced to thought encapsulated within the living organ that played and played night and day.

Day and night I called out within myself for love to match the hunger of my starving world.

The collapse of childhood, the rising from the ashes.

Tell me now, where is the fire, where has it gone?

The heat dissipating into my darkness and I was frozen again within memory – but somehow embedded within sun and moon and sky.

What had changed me? Who was it who had called out from beyond me? What was their name? How did they know me?

The protective film covering my heart pierced by love's many losses, as I was swept away by sorrow's undercurrent to another place.

O far shore, in the waters my shoulders shed the burden of the years, as I coated my own heart – for you, this time.

Gift-wrapped, shielded from the war raging at battle's edge.

It is for you, my darling – O how you dazzled me.

It was such a sudden appearing within the inner sanctum.

God and man in colour, contour and content to peel away the concrete forms of day.

Encoding the silence of the present moment in which formation advances upwards.

And downwards I cast my bread upon the waters of my consciousness.

Downwards I fell, staying so still upon the stone, eyes closed – only listening left.

Who comes? For whom am I waiting in this solitary place?

Footfalls longed for – such measured steps, I hardly dare look up.

Lifted up, taken in, as I receive a piece of the mystery within the circle of your gaze.

And beholding and beheld – O how you wounded me, but I was wounded already – so far from complete.

Beloved, think on in swift movements of the hand – dreaming still.

The first light of the first day has dawned upon the firstborn as I whisper – 'I will.'

drawn / pierced / unseen

drawn

the sting sucked out
and swallowed
deep-throated love
deep darkness
born in the bearing
of sin in one body
crowned with thorns
where, o death, is your victory?
where, o death, is your sting?
it is drawn
sucked out
swallowed
deep-throated love
in the deep darkness
expressed in the descent
down and down
to where
i am
found

pierced

rain piercing through night's darkness
giant tears expressing heaven's remorse
hard, dry hearts beat down
so much of the earth's great potential
someone's blood tonight stains the grey city stone
and i sit alone within walls of my own making
silence and sun, doors and a waiting world
stepping out, hands to wring out every wrong
today the wind blows across my face
and it is enough, the piercing drives me on

unseen

the greater miracle
exists in spirit space
threading through the ether
golden threads –
the assurance, the conviction
the absolute certainty that is faith

drawn out of the mist
pierced now the heart of darkness
unseen between worlds

it comes like a sword
to touch the edge of my soul
light and darkness divide

peace thrown like a bomb
into the heart of the war
exploding within

the pieces scatter
seeds in distressed soil to grow
morning's victory

beauty burns

beauty burns
truth shadows
goodness testifies
[that faith without works
is dead]

set alight
keep rendering
she is there

the unseen essence
ever waiting to step
into newly created forms

she is
the soul
of the masterpiece

touching hers
means to touch
yours

grace-filled she arches
her slender neck:
her swan song

her first
and last
sound

rises
like smoke
dissipating within

and then silence
penetrating my dusk
my dawn

kiss me now

kiss me now
now that the drops of water
on the window pane have dried
and weeping has ceased

kiss me now
now that the leaves have fallen
the birds have flown
and the winter has settled in

kiss me now
now that the bearing cannot be borne
the burden cannot be lifted
and the flight to the desert is complete

kiss me now
now that it is dark and it's late
the pathway is deserted and the plants
hang their heads in shame

kiss me now
now that the depths are deeper
the heights higher and God's love stronger
than we ever could have imagined

kiss me now
now that the last person has gone
and there are no witnesses left to see
how the sun had so burned me

kiss me now
now that the day will not last long
now that the night will be even shorter
now that eyes are heavy with sleep

kiss me now
now that the drops . . .
. . . have dried
and weeping . . . ceased

Far

The garden overlooking the sea
The grassy path leading down to the road
Those sunsets, the clear evenings
Such long summers, the stretch of golden beach
Rock upon rock in the dazzling heat
Became as shadows on my childish soul

And I see again clearly the landscape of aloneness
It is like a cold knife touching my skin
But never pierced, I travelled far
And so far on now, I cannot look back and see
That small figure carving shapes in the sand
Without the fingers of my hand clutching at the urban air

I was lost with you and without you
My story, my dream, my words, my companions
Were figments affecting me but never touching me
Never replacing the cold steel of the knife
That always threatened to draw blood
If I took one step too far

Today you are all gone, all of you
Vanished like the sea mist of the morning
Sometimes upon the ocean within me
A wave rises and I think I see your primeval figure
Riding the crest, but it soon disappears into the deep
And the surface flattens out into eternity

The house is still there, the beds, the curtains, the covers
All the same; and the nights, the walking, the long, long days
Have all merged and melted away
I recall only the smallest details now
But I want this poem not to end
I want you not to be gone from those old, old places

Even though the distance is too far
Even though I cannot go back to find her
She remains with me under the shadow of that great rock
The sea filling her eyes like tears, glassy green
Waiting, waiting and watching for the wave that would break
Over her heart – the one to cast her upon another shore

the hills are shrouded in mist

the hills are shrouded in mist
the path is clear
welcome is at the door
my love, please come home

o in such a dark night was the dark fire lit from within
burning as the hours deepened – my heart growing colder towards
    sunrise

losing sight of You meant i was no longer visible to myself
without walls – without bounds – without union

without what i was becoming held in our hands
i lower my eyes – in such a dark night the dark fire was to give no warmth,
    no light

This Year

This year I will let the wind blow through the cracks and the rain soak the
    dry ground
This year I will let the river run its course and the sea wash over me
This year I will learn a different kind of seeing and practise the language of
    the spirit
This year I will stand and survey the landscape from the highest of vantage
    points
This year I will be the first one to rise as if from the ashes and burst into a
    sudden strong flame
This year I will let the Word be a dividing sword
This year I will behold the Lord

I see through a glass darkly

I see through a glass darkly
I see the pale light filtering through the bedroom blind
I see myself in the mirror
The reflection hanging in the air like dust before settling

I see through a glass darkly
I see figures in the street always moving away
I see shop windows reflecting the illusion of happiness
And I glimpse myself moving swiftly on
The image of my face vanishing into the fading light of day

I see in part
I do not see enough
I see as a child the abiding of the three
Faith, Hope and Love, but the greatest is He
Who holds the promise perfect of all I could be

Fully known
I shall know fully
No shadow cast
Light that will last

Known fully
Fully shall I know
Healed
Revealed
Nothing concealed

If I were a poet ...

If I were a poet
I would press a word into your hand
As I shook it and ask: How are you?
Smiling, the truth would not be spoken:

Last summer there were many days I shivered in the noonday heat
Spring only blossomed on the very edges of my seeing
Winter froze me quietly
Autumn felled me softly
And the earth's earth buried my heart

But the song, the song went on
Gliding through the night like a ship on dark waters
Leaving golden threads in its wake
Weaving through the days that rolled on and on
Like wave after wave breaking on the silver shore

If I were a poet
I would enter the furnace of forgetfulness
And the maelstrom of memory
In order to remember and record what you would not, could not
I would let the heat of your unuttered words sear me
And the whirlwind of your storms spin me

If I were a poet
I would record your dignity as an eagle's first flight
Your hunger as a burning tree:
The charred branches of your arms reaching out to receive
This year's harvest

If I were a poet
I would write what I heard you cry, shout, speak
Whisper and whimper before your dying breath
Misted up the window pane
What would I write with my finger?
It would be your name

If I were a poet
If I were wholly the world's possession
If my meanings were as drops of water on your parched lips
If my metaphors carried over a bundle of new life to you
If my meter caused you to fall in step with my Master
I would write and write

On through the dark contemplation
On as the dark fire burned
On as the silver and gold threaded through your soul's darkest night
On until sunrise kissed your eyes with the morning's first light

a house made of wood

there it is in the woods
a house made of the same
tree, trunk, bark, branch
cut down, sawn through
sawdust lifted up
and scattered
by the winds of every season
material of the earth taken
to make
a shelter, a resting place
in which to ignite the fire
and burn
in which to let the light in after dark
and learn

The City Sounded

The city sounded two voices
One filled with the ideal self
Questing and finding and fulfilling
All sorts of highly visible desires

The other talking only to self
The homeless man people choose not to see
Worn and weary he sits by me
Speaking over all sorts of shrouded desires

It is an incomprehensible murmur
Here is the city's shadow
Its unacknowledged madness
Lurking within the man no one will look in the eye

Can I look backwards to see what he was
Or forwards to what he will become?
The other voice sounds over the top
Of this ever-present soundtrack

So few people hear it but it rises up
In the nightmares of the respectable
In every act of urban violence
In every instance of self-loathing

It is unconscious and so dangerous
Perpetual and so powerful
It confirms the rich in their identity
Covers the insecure in their vulnerability

The city sounded two voices
I heard both as I sat by the man without a home
I held his gaze only for a few seconds
And was wounded by his insanity

I left him talking to himself
Drinking the coffee he purchased
That made him equal with me
I turn and see him looking through the glass

Our eyes searching space
For home or a place to hide?
The city sounded two voices tonight
And as I advance into the neon light

The murmur of his words rest
Upon the swell of an inner tide
But as I walk on they slip down
Disappearing for ever into a soundless deep

Blind alley or infinity?

Was I led or did I blunder my way here?
Guided or side-tracked?
My hand against the brick
My back against the wall
Proximity only to self
Or infinity?
No ideas ...
The sky above me
The earth below me
A wall in front of me
The past behind me
Rooted to the spot
Nowhere to go
Eyes closed
To see the universe
Emptied of home

Taken, Blessed, Broken, Given

Betrayal and denial at the door.

Taking the bread,

Saying thank you despite

Touching the edges of such a dark night;

Breaking the loaf,

And giving the pieces away.

Morsels pressed into hungry palms,

Your words resounding still:

Take it, this is my body . . .

The sins of the world at the door.

You took the cup that would not pass,

Saying thank you despite

The deepening darkness all around;

You gave it to those that you called friends.

The circle breaking

As trembling fingers clasped the chalice,

Your words resounding still:

This is my blood of the covenant,

Which is poured out for many . . .

For the ways that we betray you,

For the times that we deny you,

Help us to receive all that is still

Given from your nail-pierced hands.

Bread of heaven came down,

Fruit of the vine poured out,

Feed us and fill us, O Lord

In both the blessing of life and its cost;

Thanking you in every season,

Our hands open

Ready to clasp the cup as it passes by us.

Lifecycle

A stone falling to the ground
A cloud moving across the sun
– *Moonlight* –

The crest of the wave
The sand on the shore
– *Wisdom* –

The shade of the tree
Raindrops on the grass
  Birdsong –

A dream in the dark
A light in the morning
– *Sympathy* –

A touch of the hand
A beat of the heart
– *Knowledge* –

The passing of time
The losing of love
– *Silence* –

This is the time for poetry . . .

This is the time for poetry . . .
The young man in the café
On the next table to me and my closest poetry friend
Sat penning verse
Line after line in swift movements of the hand
I glanced over every now and then
As my friend and I talked pure poetry –
From where it had taken us, until now

And then there was the businessman
Next to me on the bus homeward
He sat swiftly scanning line after line
I strained to see the book's title
The Wrecking Light

I watched his suited reflection in the front window
Of the double-decker
His hands slowly turning the pages
As if searching for green shoots
To appear between the concrete cracks of his day

I got out three A4 sheets of my most recent poems
Which were folded in my handbag
And read them – our shoulders almost touching

I looked it up *The Wrecking Light* when I got home
And, oh my . . . brilliant but unrelentingly bleak was the consensus –
A sign of the times

This is the time for poetry . . .
This is the time to find
The rhyme and the rhythm

This is the time for poetry . . .
When smallness presses us
Into the darkest of corners
When disappointments plummet
One after the other
Into the hidden pool of our souls

This is the time for poetry …
The seed that slips down the concrete crack
Does not die

This is the time for poetry …
Poetry will find the unattended part of you
And blow the dust away

The Widow's Surplus

Bereaved as I was for these many years
Comfort grew as I leaned heavenwards
And now so late in life learning
From the man they called Master
Listening to his words fall like drops of pure water
Onto my parched ears
And trickle down into my heart
I would go and hear him, rain or shine
Poor as I was, with no man to lean upon
Except this one
Wherever he went
Rivers of people surged round him
He was water from a rock
And I lived in a desert
With a hardened people
But now forgiveness flourished
Green shoots of healing pushed up through
Stony ground
Deliverance was demonstrated time after time
Each step of his imprinting the earth with God's footprint
I would move out of my widow's house whenever he was near
I'd travel too, because when I thought all love had died
My widow's heart glowed warm again
My widow's clenched hand wanted to reach out
But what did I have?
What could I offer the Owner of all?
The Master had never seen me

Knew not my name
But today when I woke from my widow's sleep
My thoughts were full of him as I emptied my purse –
A sign of my unending trust
God in me – me in God, I knew not
I cared not for tomorrow's bread
Because today, today I was full
Today I would go to the Treasury
Rub shoulders with the rich
My one cent would drop from my opening hand
And I'd think of the Master's words from the Mount
About sparrows and lilies
Bereaved as I was, it would be something no man saw
And I'd smile through my tears
Because in that act
I'd be a widow no more

Mark 12 vs 41–44

Evensong

I walk upon the ancient stone
I bend towards words to peer into meanings beneath the one shown
I wait for silence to engulf the day's end
I remain in the darkness not remembering anything at all
I stand alone

My love
The birds are flown

I see figures scurry away to hiding places deep within the city walls
I look upon today's intentions threading through my actions with no way
    back
I hear a whispering tonight weaving through the branches of my mind

Weeping will not cease in this life
The dark night is long
Upon my arm now rest
Strive in all things for completeness

There is a dark cloud 35,000 feet above Europe

There is a dark cloud 35,000 feet above Europe
And an eerie calm
The wind has vanished
The planes aren't flying
The volcano's spewing
Dust and ash into the atmosphere above our heads
[But no one is mourning]
No one is asking for the mysterious mighty breath
To blow the dark cloud west

There is a dark cloud 35,000 feet above Europe
And it's not going away
The build-up of pressure from the land of ice
Is now too much – and, oh my
[The debt cannot be borne]
An eruption: the northern land is an angry man
Casting his shadow on those with more money in their pockets
While the countless nameless die daily in the south
A mighty interruption ensues . . .

. . . A journey through five countries
Eleven hours, light and night
A city break, station and motion
Countless nameless people scrabbling to get back home
Queries, tickets and stuff, and hours and hours of news
Counting the cost and the ripping off
And no parliament, no union, no summit
No one who has the power to say, enough is enough!
There is a dark cloud 35,000 feet above Europe

Today in Brussels from the window of a slowly moving train
I saw nearly naked woman after woman posing in shop after shop
    window
I was on my way to the El Greco exhibition
Where I would consider in the gallery's artificial light his masterpiece
The Disrobing of Christ
Red light, broad daylight, the night is a narrow field to be buried alive in
The turning of wheels on the railway track seemed to beat out the lie

[There is no wrong, it matters not]
As the ticket touts, the bankers, the people-traffickers all proudly line up

On my way back I see them still bending and swaying behind the glass
And, oh my [no one is mourning]
The eerie calm deepens
The dust and ash descends
For God's sake Europeans, let us look up!
And ask for the mysterious breath
To cancel the debt
And blow the dark mighty cloud
As far as the east is from the west

My dream of you is a daydream

My dream of you
is a daydream /
It is filled with light /
Intelligence sparks /
Small fires are lit
to keep us warm
when it's dark

what will be emboldened as the blossom falls?

enfolded now
now it's getting late
and the thread tightens

people hurry home
scurry along streets
seeking creatures that they are

i am being moved
sometimes slowly / sometimes not
breaking open / closing tight shut

it matters not
it matters not
we come and we go

we go and return
and always see the same
yet not i yet not

what has changed?
what have i become?
what will be emboldened

as the blossom falls?
and it is my destiny to fall
a loosening grip . . .

fragment
of the mystery
that i am

o, my darling
the still point
of tragedy

it has
a
silent core

[the wind
bends
the bough]

abide there
my love
encode the silence

until
you are
no more

I wait in the garden for my beloved

I wait in the garden for my beloved
Planes pass by overhead
And what has been said cannot be unsaid
No recalling as the blossom falls
No recalling as the blossom falls
The birds call and call
Carried on the gentle breeze
The scent of memories
Fragrant and fragile
Fragile and perfectly still
Everything I do will be for you
Everything I do will be for you
The fountain flows and flows
The birds call and call
Planes pass by overhead
And what has been said my love
Cannot be unsaid

wish list

a walk
in the park
an hour
or two
before
it gets
dark

guest of my soul

to carry the night
to slip through the cracks
to wait for my returning
to keep on the light

carry over

let the music carry the sound
sound will carry the sadness
sadness will carry the memory
memory will carry the movement
cast back <
thrust forward >
as the river runs on
as the river runs on

vista

the landscape
is before us /
time and eternity
flowing from
our hands /
as the sand
slips through
our various
fingers

Prophecy

For Cyprian Norwid

There was no one
A human void left you voiceless
Save the seeping history pouring from your eyes
The creeping mystery flowing from your hands
Startling Poetry blinking into the day's light …
Penniless and alone
You were right about only your son's son
Reading you aright
Vanished in a pauper's grave
The poet turns, for
The poet knew
The stones that I would step upon today
– The people's hands are indeed swollen with applause –

The benevolent nineteenth-century idols of progress and mass propaganda, the righteous makers of ideology, have turned into twentieth-century monsters whose presence [Norwid] sensed and tried to exorcise through his poetry. He was not a romantic visionary, he reacted with his intellect and irony against the romantic prognostications: time, past and present, was for him like the silent links in human communication, an interlocking continuum. What is bypassed in the continuum of the present will be retraced in a future sequence: for the future is, as Norwid calls it, 'the eternal corrector'.

From The Other Side of Silence – The Poet at the Limit of Language *by*
Jerzy Peterkiewicz

The cross planted; the garden in darkness

My soul rises and falls
Rises to God and fails to grasp hold
And so falls

I remember the hard things as I pour out my soul within me
Of oneness and aloneness and singularity

In times past I blinked in the sun's bright light
Then, the sun was high in the sky
Then, the sun illuminated all it touched

What do I say to my soul in despair?
'Time is slipping through my fingers, so please
Stand upright'

I remember the cross, planted
I remember the garden, in darkness

I close my eyes
I begin to whisper
And a wave breaks over me

The Lord says, 'It is enough now, enough'

I say, 'My falling is circled within your dying
Why is it so clear to me?
My vision increases, as my strength diminishes ...'

Yes, I know there is a foe
For he is robbing me

What do I say to my soul in despair?
'Time is slipping through my fingers, so please
Stand upright'

fragments

I

take me there now
now the wind whispers low
now that the boat waits
rocking to and fro
like an empty cradle

take me there now
now it's calm
the days are long
and the lullaby
has become a song

2

sound of the sea
— ancestry —

pull of the tide
— inside —

birds calling to each other
— mother —

great rocks standing in time
— sublime —

quietness of an ageing hand
— sand —

a gentle breeze across my face
— embrace —

3

starlight shoots through my heart
its shards filling my eyes tonight
from now on I will cry tears
of everlasting light

love-sick

staring space;
the un-melted heart's
only object
an inner face

love of my love

love of my love
in whose gaze I will live
my book of hours to you I give

hallowed hollowness

hollow vessel
empty unless filled
brimming over unless poured out
[whose hands will clasp?
whose face will turn
eyes caught by the glint
of light refracted upwards
from the glass?]
liquid love ripples
fingers tremble
one sip and
the heart's knowledge
of the head
the head's understanding
of the heart
will be tasted
and slip down into hollowness
this hallowed evening
drink deep
only one hand-span of time is left
completion waits at the door

In the age we live in cosmic symbolism has been almost forgotten and submerged under a tidal wave of trademarks, political party buttons, advertising and propaganda slogans and all the rest – is necessarily an age of mass psychosis. A world in which a poet can find practically no material in the common substance of everyday life, and in which he is driven crazy in his search for the vital symbols that have been buried alive under a mountain of cultural garbage, can only end up . . . in self-destruction. And that is why some of the best poets of our time are running wild among the tombs in the moonlit cemeteries of surrealism. Faithful to the instincts of the true poet, they are unable to seek their symbols save in the depths of the spirit where these symbols are found. These depths have become a ruin and a slum. But poetry must, and does, make good use of whatever it finds there: starvation, madness, frustration and death.

Thomas Merton, Bread in the Wilderness

Evening Vespers

I sat surrounded by stone and the tombs of the poets reminding me to search the ruins for the symbols buried under the rubble in the depth of the spirit.

History underfoot and the tremor of the organ playing the notes of ancient songs with voices rising and candles flickering reminding me of heaven – heartbreak's home.

Surrounded by stone – eyes cast down – prayers rising and falling as the light outside weakens into darkness and so many shadowy figures waiting waiting waiting for a benediction or a sign.

But oh it's late – inward motion is stilled and who wants to know or remember or examine the failure of love as the incense swirls and swirls round the tomb of a long-dead saint?

Made right? Made light under the glare of the camera – and there was Christ dying within me again, and oh where was I? Under the tombs of the poets – half sane half mad;

And afterwards in the twilight outside calling to the moon for a turning of the tide and a revelation of how deep is the darkness – how high are the walls – how low is the tide – and how love waits waits waits . . .

17 September 2010, Westminster Abbey

It comes

It comes from within
It comes in the night
It comes and breaks the circle
It comes at a price
It comes with a kiss
It comes with lanterns
It comes with swords
It comes in a ravine
It comes despite the offer of bread
It comes because Satan entered
It comes and buys a field to bury itself
It comes and counts silver pieces
It comes and throws the silver pieces down
It comes and remorse is only a knife
It comes and confesses to the merciless
It comes and fatally wounds itself
It comes and strangles all life

Apostate / Thief
Betrayer / Disciple
Son / Brother

What did you hear that last fateful night?

Lies as truth
Truth as condemnation
Condemnation as rationalisation
Rationalisation as right

Who owes what to whom?
What does it matter?

As the Lord lived
He loved

As the Lord died
His clothes were divided
Won in a game
Thrown lots

As the Lord lives
He loves

He releases God's holy dove

It comes from above
It comes from above
It comes from above

One Three Nine

I searched, I did
I know many things, I do
My thoughts are close to me, so close
Flames searing my innermost parts
Sitting down, arising
The flames of thought burn and burn
The scrutinised path, the bed I lie upon so singed
Intimately acquainted with the worded tongue
I am enclosed
My hand laid upon the plough, it trembles
The knowledge of you high-beamed above me, unattained
Where can I go? Rooted to the spot
Or winged, dawn breaks me down
What remains unshaken? How I am led?
Darkness and light alike, intertwined in the inward part
Woven in Mother's womb
Fearfully wonderfully worked
Exposed frame skilfully wrought
O, my unformed substance has formed an outer shell
And I cannot see the days ordained
Nor what is written in your book:
You say, there is a hurtful and an everlasting way
And the heart is to be searched for anxious thoughts most dear
And that on the wings of dawn, the choice is clear

Psalm 139

love enough, enough love

the heart's desire flickers
like an unsure candle in an uncertain breeze

what was it you said about
a smouldering wick? tell me please

how can i keep burning when the day covers my longing
and the nights are so very short?
. . .

today your words
alighted in me

on the wing of birdsong
on the sure, sure wind of morning

'my love, the fuel for the fire
is the locus of your desire'
. . .

the air of your spirit
the wood of your cross

Saviour, Lord
'enough', you say, 'enough'

Thought-fragment

Seen beyond the surface
Surfaced after a long time
Timed attack for ultimate damage
Damaged but touched by love
Loved towards nightfall
Falling towards You

The inescapable Good
The indescribable Beauty
The indestructible Truth